HAL•LEONARD®

TRUMPET
PLAY-ALONG

AUDIO
ACCESS
INCLUDED

GREAT THEMES

VOL. 4

To access audio visit:
www.halleonard.com/mylibrary

Enter Code
3534-0146-0424-0752

ISBN 978-1-4950-0014-0

Visit Hal Leonard Online at
www.halleonard.com

HAL•LEONARD®
CORPORATION
7777 W. BLUEMOUND RD. P.O. BOX 13819
MILWAUKEE, WISCONSIN 53213

GREAT THEMES

CONTENTS

Cherry Pink and Apple Blossom White

from UNDERWATER

French Words by Jacques Larue
English Words by Mack David
Music by Marcel Louiguy

Deborah's Theme

from ONCE UPON A TIME IN AMERICA

By Ennio Morricone

Dragnet

Words and Music by Walter Schumann and Miklos Rosza

* *All chords played over timpani pattern (D-G-D-G).*

The Godfather Waltz

from the Paramount Pictures THE GODFATHER, GODFATHER II, and GODFATHER III
By Nino Rota

*Trumpet part is performed without any accompaniment.
**Play-along track starts here.

Gonna Fly Now

Theme from ROCKY

By Bill Conti, Ayn Robbins and Carol Connors

Green Hornet Theme

By Billy May

The Odd Couple

Theme from the Paramount Television Series THE ODD COUPLE

By Neal Hefti

Sugar Lips

Words and Music by Billy Sherrill and Buddy Killen

HAL•LEONARD® TRUMPET PLAY-ALONG

The Trumpet Play-Along Series will help you play your favorite songs quickly and easily. Just follow the printed music, listen to the sound-alike recordings and hear how the trumpet should sound, and then play along using the separate backing tracks.

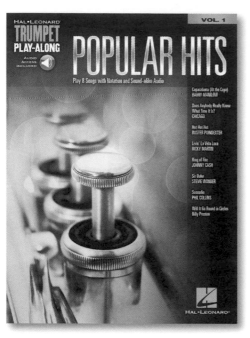

1. POPULAR HITS
Copacabana (At the Copa) (Barry Manilow) • Does Anybody Really Know What Time It Is? (Chicago) • Hot Hot Hot (Buster Poindexter) • Livin' La Vida Loca (Ricky Martin) • Ring of Fire (Johnny Cash) • Sir Duke (Stevie Wonder) • Sussudio (Phil Collins) • Will It Go Round in Circles (Billy Preston).

00137383
Book/Online Audio
$16.99

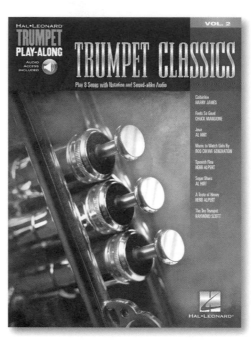

2. TRUMPET CLASSICS
Ciribiribin (Harry James) • Feels So Good (Chuck Mangione) • Java (Al Hirt) • Music to Watch Girls By (Bob Crewe Generation) • Spanish Flea (Herb Alpert) • Sugar Blues (Al Hirt) • A Taste of Honey (Herb Alpert) • The Toy Trumpet (Raymond Scott).

00137384
Book/Online Audio
$16.99

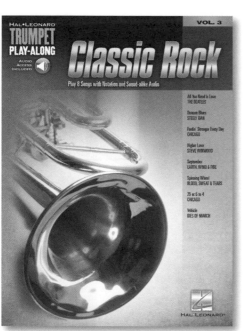

3. CLASSIC ROCK
All You Need Is Love (The Beatles) • Deacon Blues (Steely Dan) • Feelin' Stronger Every Day (Chicago) • Higher Love (Steve Winwood) • September (Earth, Wind & Fire) • Spinning Wheel (Blood, Sweat & Tears) • 25 or 6 to 4 (Chicago) • Vehicle (Ides of March).

00137385
Book/Online Audio
$16.99

4. GREAT THEMES
Cherry Pink and Apple Blossom White (Perez Prado) • Deborah's Theme (Ennio Morricone) • Dragnet (Walter Schumann) • The Godfather Waltz (Nino Rota) • Gonna Fly Now (Bill Conti) • Green Hornet Theme (Al Hirt) • The Odd Couple (Neal Hefti) • Sugar Lips (Al Hirt).

00137386
Book/Online Audio
$16.99

HAL•LEONARD®
CORPORATION
7777 W. BLUEMOUND RD. P.O. BOX 13819 MILWAUKEE, WI 53213

Prices, contents, and availability subject to change without notice.

www.halleonard.com

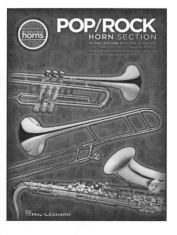

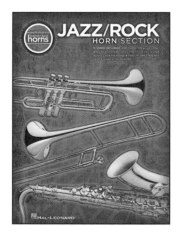

HAL•LEONARD INSTRUMENTAL PLAY-ALONG

Your favorite songs are arranged just for solo instrumentalists with this outstanding series. Each book includes a great full-accompaniment play-along CD so you can sound just like a pro! Check out www.halleonard.com to see all the titles available.

Disney Greats

Arabian Nights • Hawaiian Roller Coaster Ride • It's a Small World • Look Through My Eyes • Yo Ho (A Pirate's Life for Me) • and more.

_____ 00841934	Flute	$12.95
_____ 00841935	Clarinet	$12.95
_____ 00841936	Alto Sax	$12.95
_____ 00841937	Tenor Sax	$12.95
_____ 00841938	Trumpet	$12.95
_____ 00841939	Horn	$12.95
_____ 00841940	Trombone	$12.95
_____ 00841941	Violin	$12.95
_____ 00841942	Viola	$12.95
_____ 00841943	Cello	$12.95
_____ 00842078	Oboe	$12.95

Glee

And I Am Telling You I'm Not Going • Defying Gravity • Don't Stop Believin' • Keep Holding On • Lean on Me • No Air • Sweet Caroline • True Colors • and more.

_____ 00842479	Flute	$12.99
_____ 00842480	Clarinet	$12.99
_____ 00842481	Alto Sax	$12.99
_____ 00842482	Tenor Sax	$12.99
_____ 00842483	Trumpet	$12.99
_____ 00842484	Horn	$12.99
_____ 00842485	Trombone	$12.99
_____ 00842486	Violin	$12.99
_____ 00842487	Viola	$12.99
_____ 00842488	Cello	$12.99

Motown Classics

ABC • Endless Love • I Just Called to Say I Love You • My Girl • The Tracks of My Tears • What's Going On • You've Really Got a Hold on Me • and more.

_____ 00842572	Flute	$12.99
_____ 00842573	Clarinet	$12.99
_____ 00842574	Alto Saxophone	$12.99
_____ 00842575	Tenor Saxophone	$12.99
_____ 00842576	Trumpet	$12.99
_____ 00842577	Horn	$12.99
_____ 00842578	Trombone	$12.99
_____ 00842579	Violin	$12.99
_____ 00842580	Viola	$12.99
_____ 00842581	Cello	$12.99

Popular Hits

Breakeven • Fireflies • Halo • Hey, Soul Sister • I Gotta Feeling • I'm Yours • Need You Now • Poker Face • Viva La Vida • You Belong with Me • and more.

_____ 00842511	Flute	$12.99
_____ 00842512	Clarinet	$12.99
_____ 00842513	Alto Sax	$12.99
_____ 00842514	Tenor Sax	$12.99
_____ 00842515	Trumpet	$12.99
_____ 00842516	Horn	$12.99
_____ 00842517	Trombone	$12.99
_____ 00842518	Violin	$12.99
_____ 00842519	Viola	$12.99
_____ 00842520	Cello	$12.99

Sports Rock

Another One Bites the Dust • Centerfold • Crazy Train • Get Down Tonight • Let's Get It Started • Shout • The Way You Move • and more.

_____ 00842326	Flute	$12.99
_____ 00842327	Clarinet	$12.99
_____ 00842328	Alto Sax	$12.99
_____ 00842329	Tenor Sax	$12.99
_____ 00842330	Trumpet	$12.99
_____ 00842331	Horn	$12.99
_____ 00842332	Trombone	$12.99
_____ 00842333	Violin	$12.99
_____ 00842334	Viola	$12.99
_____ 00842335	Cello	$12.99

Women of Pop

Bad Romance • Jar of Hearts • Mean • My Life Would Suck Without You • Our Song • Rolling in the Deep • Single Ladies (Put a Ring on It) • Teenage Dream • and more.

_____ 00842650	Flute	$12.99
_____ 00842651	Clarinet	$12.99
_____ 00842652	Alto Sax	$12.99
_____ 00842653	Tenor Sax	$12.99
_____ 00842654	Trumpet	$12.99
_____ 00842655	Horn	$12.99
_____ 00842656	Trombone	$12.99
_____ 00842657	Violin	$12.99
_____ 00842658	Viola	$12.99
_____ 00842659	Cello	$12.99

Twilight

Bella's Lullaby • Decode • Eyes on Fire • Full Moon • Go All the Way (Into the Twilight) • Leave Out All the Rest • Spotlight (Twilight Remix) • Supermassive Black Hole • Tremble for My Beloved.

_____ 00842406	Flute	$12.99
_____ 00842407	Clarinet	$12.99
_____ 00842408	Alto Sax	$12.99
_____ 00842409	Tenor Sax	$12.99
_____ 00842410	Trumpet	$12.99
_____ 00842411	Horn	$12.99
_____ 00842412	Trombone	$12.99
_____ 00842413	Violin	$12.99
_____ 00842414	Viola	$12.99
_____ 00842415	Cello	$12.99

Twilight – New Moon

Almost a Kiss • Dreamcatcher • Edward Leaves • I Need You • Memories of Edward • New Moon • Possibility • Roslyn • Satellite Heart • and more.

_____ 00842458	Flute	$12.99
_____ 00842459	Clarinet	$12.99
_____ 00842460	Alto Sax	$12.99
_____ 00842461	Tenor Sax	$12.99
_____ 00842462	Trumpet	$12.99
_____ 00842463	Horn	$12.99
_____ 00842464	Trombone	$12.99
_____ 00842465	Violin	$12.99
_____ 00842466	Viola	$12.99
_____ 00842467	Cello	$12.99

Wicked

As Long As You're Mine • Dancing Through Life • Defying Gravity • For Good • I'm Not That Girl • Popular • The Wizard and I • and more.

_____ 00842236	Book/CD Pack	$11.95
_____ 00842237	Book/CD Pack	$11.95
_____ 00842238	Alto Saxophone	$11.95
_____ 00842239	Tenor Saxophone	$11.95
_____ 00842240	Trumpet	$11.95
_____ 00842241	Horn	$11.95
_____ 00842242	Trombone	$11.95
_____ 00842243	Violin	$11.95
_____ 00842244	Viola	$11.95
_____ 00842245	Cello	$11.95

FOR MORE INFORMATION, SEE YOUR LOCAL MUSIC DEALER, OR WRITE TO:

HAL•LEONARD® CORPORATION

7777 W. BLUEMOUND RD. P.O. BOX 13819 MILWAUKEE, WI 53213